A "Read, America!" classic

The How Rude!™ Handbook of

School Manners for Teens

Civility in the Hallowed Halls

The **How Rude!**™ **Handbook of**

School Manners for Teens

Civility in the Hallowed Halls

Alex J. Packer, Ph.D.

Edited by Pamela Espeland

free spirit
PUBLiSHiNG®

Helping kids
help themselves™
since 1983

Free Spirit, Free Spirit Publishing, and associated logos are trademarks and/or registered trademarks of Free Spirit Publishing Inc. A complete listing of our logos and trademarks is available at *www.freespirit.com.*

Library of Congress Cataloging-in-Publication Data
Packer, Alex J.
    The how rude! handbook of school manners for teens : civility in the hallowed halls / Alex J. Packer ; edited by Pamela Espeland.
        p. cm. — (The how rude handbooks for teens)
    Includes index.
    ISBN 1-57542-164-X
    1. Students—Conduct of life. 2. Teenagers—Conduct of life. 3. Ethics. I. Espeland, Pamela. II. Title. III. Series.
    BJ1661.P23 2004
    395.5—dc22   2004018972

Cover design by Marieka Heinlen
Interior design by Percolator
Illustrations by Jeff Tolbert
Index prepared by Ina Gravitz

10 9 8 7 6 5 4 3 2
Printed in the United States of America

Free Spirit Publishing Inc.
217 Fifth Avenue North, Suite 200
Minneapolis, MN 55401-1299
(612) 338-2068
help4kids@freespirit.com
www.freespirit.com

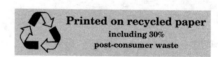
Printed on recycled paper
including 30%
post-consumer waste

CONTENTS

CAUTION!

This is a book about manners.

If that makes you feel like a dog being trotted off to obedience school, at least say "Excuse me" before barking during morning announcements.

INTRODUCTION

Imagine a place where stressed-out teens compete for grades, popularity, and the last can of soda in the vending machine. Where you're expected to take tests, turn in homework, and dissect frogs. Where you start the day by walking through a metal detector and end it by running for a bus.

It's called *school*.

People wonder why there isn't more politeness in schools. How much politeness can there be in a place where toilet stalls have no doors? Where, every 43  minutes, you get bowled over by a million stampeding sneakers? Where chalk squeaks and bells blare and no one ever seems to care?

It's a miracle there's as much politeness in schools as there is. But there needs to be *more*. Why? Because teenagers spend more of their waking day in school than anyplace else. And they deserve a school climate that's safe, respectful, and friendly.

The *climate* of a school is what it feels like to be there. The better a school's climate is, the more likely its students are to enjoy school, do well academically, behave morally, and stay out of trouble. Schools with outstanding climates have many things in common, including:

- a prideful sense of community
- clearly stated values
- high expectations for student behavior and achievement
- respect for the needs and feelings of others
- close student-teacher relationships, and
- creamed corn for lunch every Tuesday

In the best schools—schools that students enjoy attending and do well in—people are polite to one another.

Unfortunately, this is rare and getting rarer.

The Rise of School Rudeness

To find out the state of manners in schools today, we surveyed teachers and students.

When we asked teachers, "Do you think students today are more polite, less polite, or the same as when you were growing up?" 75 percent said, "Less polite."

When we asked, "How do you feel about the manners and social behaviors of the students you teach?" 56 percent said, "Very disappointed," or "Disappointed."

Rude Things Students Do (According to Teachers)

When we asked teachers, "What rude things do students do to you?" these were the top 10 answers:

1. Talk while I'm trying to teach.
2. Not raise their hand.
3. Not say "Please," "Thank you," and "Excuse me."
4. Talk back.
5. Make no attempt to hide their boredom, irritation, or anger.
6. Not pay attention.
7. Use physical or verbal aggression to get their way.
8. Swear.
9. Keep doing something after being asked to stop.
10. Use disrespectful body language (roll their eyes, slouch, etc.).

When we asked, "What rude things do students do to each other?" these were the top 15 answers:

1. Say mean things.
2. Call each other names.
3. Taunt each other.
4. Pick one to blame for everything.
5. Make fun of each other.
6. Whisper about someone behind his or her back.
7. Trip each other in the hallways.

continues...

8. Dump their books.

9. Fight with each other.

10. Exclude each other.

11. Fail to apologize to each other.

12. Invade each other's space.

13. Interfere with each other's education.

14. Refuse to tolerate anything that isn't the status quo.

15. Pass gas.

These teachers weren't just dumping on kids. The same proportion (75 percent) who said that students today are less polite also said that *adults* are less polite today than they were a generation ago. As one teacher put it:

> "I don't think ANY of us spend enough time teaching manners and politeness."

Another teacher said:

> "Schools and students today are but a reflection of society's tolerance for lower standards of behavior."

Before you say, "See, it's not our fault!" keep in mind that soon *you'll* be the adults. So it's up to *you* to raise the standards.

About This Book

You can't change the slackers, snoozers, and delinquents at your school into courteous learners. But you can be a shining example. Someone others look up to and want to be like. Someone who is admired by students and beloved by teachers.

This book is a backpack-sized course on school politeness. It makes up for the fact that most student handbooks don't cover manners. If you look in your handbook, you'll probably find all kinds of information about attendance policies, discipline policies, homework policies, and dress codes. But where's the dirt on dealing with cheaters? On handling bullies? On coping with crushes on teachers? Right here, along with more advice on everyday etiquette in the educational environment.

Think of this book as your politeness policy. Your school manners manual. Your courtesy code.

Good luck, and good manners!

Alex Packer
Boston, Massachusetts

 **I keep having this dream that I'm naked in school. Is this normal?**

Absolutely. In fact, one out of every three teenagers we surveyed has that very same dream. And this isn't the only school-related dream kids have. About 40 percent dream they had to take a test they didn't know about or study for. And 20 percent dream they forgot the combination to their locker. ◆

School Manners 101: Classroom Decorum

"Decorum" doesn't mean the color of the walls in the media center. It refers to those behaviors that have proven over time to encourage teaching and learning.

Like shooting spitballs, chewing gum, playing radios.... Oops, wrong list.

Like paying attention, coming to class prepared, and respecting the rights and ideas of others.

Why are good manners important in school? Because they're the first line of defense against unpleasant and illegal behavior. When people refuse to control themselves, bad things happen. In school, students are harassed, bullied, suspended, afraid, and unable to learn. In the real world, the collapse of etiquette leads to anarchy, lawsuits, and violence. Wouldn't you rather say, "Excuse me, I'm terribly sorry," than be taken to court or shot with a gun?

Rude students cost time and money. According to Public Agenda, an opinion research organization, today's teachers spend more time trying to keep order in the classroom than they do teaching students.

If your teachers spend 55 percent of their time telling kids to go back to their seats, settle down, pay attention, and stop giving each other wedgies, that means that you're getting 55 percent *less* of an education. That's a half-day of school wasted—time you could use to watch TV or play video games! Imagine how your parents would feel if they knew so much of their tax dollar was being frittered away.

Everyone benefits (except lawyers) when people are polite to one another. If you don't want etiquette to play hooky from your school, follow the code of conduct on pages 9–10. You'll be doing your part to create a warm, productive climate for students and teachers alike.

30 COMMANDMENTS
OF CLASSROOM ETIQUETTE
FOR STUDENTS

THOU SHALT...

1. listen to your teacher

2. think before you speak

3. clean up after yourself

4. come to class prepared

5. raise your hand to be called on

6. be respectful of other people's ideas

7. compliment each other

8. remove your hat in class

9. address your classmates and teachers with kindness and respect

10. keep your hands and feet to yourself

11. say "Please," "Thank you," "Excuse me," and "I'm sorry"

12. find another way besides anger to express displeasure

13. work hard in class, even if you have to pretend to be interested in a subject or assignment

14. talk directly to the person you have a conflict with, rather than to everyone else

15. remember that teachers have feelings, too

continues...

30 COMMANDMENTS
OF CLASSROOM ETIQUETTE
FOR STUDENTS

THOU SHALT NOT...

16. bully others

17. be physically or verbally aggressive

18. sexually harass others

19. ignore a reasonable request

20. talk when a teacher or classmate is talking

21. take someone else's property without permission

22. backbite or spread rumors

23. put people down to seem cool

24. interfere with each other's learning

25. act bored or fall asleep in class

26. make hurtful comments about another person's looks, abilities, background, family, religion, ethnic heritage, or sexual orientation

27. pressure others into doing things that are mean, harmful, or illegal

28. have an attitude

29. belch or pass gas on purpose

30. cause the chalk to squeak

What About Teachers?

Right now, you may be thinking, "Wait just a minute, buster. Students aren't the only rude people in school. Plenty of teachers are rude, too!"

I think you mean *"Mister"* buster—but you are right. Teachers can also be rude.

Rude Things Teachers Do (According to Teenagers)

When we asked teenagers, "What rude things do teachers do to students?" these were the top 10 answers:

1. Make fun of us in front of the whole class.

2. Ignore us on purpose.

3. Give us too much work.

4. Punish the whole class for something one person did.

5. Call on us when they know we don't have the answer.

6. Say sarcastic things.

7. Talk down to us.

8. Accuse us of doing things based on suspicion, not facts.

9. Not listen to our side of the story.

10. Play favorites.

School climate is as much about teachers' behavior as it is about students' behavior. But before we hand out their commandments, here are even more rude things students told us teachers do:

"Yell at us."

"Snap at us."

"Call us names."

"Make us feel stupid."

"Underestimate our intelligence."

"Call on certain people more than others."

"Call on boys more than girls."

"Act impatient."

"Act like they know everything."

"Assume that all teenagers act the same."

"Accuse us of cheating."

"Expect us to be on time and then arrive 20 minutes late."

"Not return our papers or tests."

"Not take the time to explain things."

"Take their crabbiness out on us."

"Judge us by our clothes or speech."

"Breathe on us with their bad breath."

"Assign busy work."

"Lose our work and blame it on us."

"Make boring lesson plans."

"Let the rest of the class know a student's grade."

"Put down our ideas."

"Think of us as 'teenagers,' not as human beings."

Eeee-youch! Teachers, are you reading this? Aren't you *shocked* by how badly some of your colleagues behave toward their students?

30 COMMANDMENTS
OF CLASSROOM ETIQUETTE
FOR TEACHERS

THOU SHALT...

1. treat all students with patience and respect

2. listen to your students

3. avoid sarcasm

4. encourage students to ask questions when they don't understand

5. take the time to explain things

6. keep your personal likes and dislikes from affecting student-teacher relationships

7. empathize with the pains and pressures of adolescence

8. treat students as individuals

9. expect the best, not the worst, from students

10. show tolerance and compassion

11. allow students to go to the bathroom

12. reward responsibility with extra privileges

13. treat boys and girls equally

14. make corny jokes at your own risk

15. use breath mints

30 COMMANDMENTS
OF CLASSROOM ETIQUETTE
FOR TEACHERS

THOU SHALT NOT...

16. ignore students

17. talk down to students

18. accuse students based only on suspicions

19. punish the whole class because of one person

20. call on students just to embarrass them

21. make fun of students in front of the whole class

22. prejudice other teachers' opinions of a student

23. invade a student's privacy

24. play favorites

25. keep students after class just to inconvenience them

26. take out your personal problems on students

27. assume the worst without letting a student offer an explanation

28. judge students before getting to know them

29. assume that all students who pass gas are doing it on purpose

30. condescend

When all students and teachers follow their Command-ments of Classroom Etiquette, schools everywhere will be more pleasant for everyone. Until that day dawns, keep reading.

Has school always been so cruel?

I don't know about "always," but it was when I was a student.

I still remember my tenth-grade math class. I tried to act invisible so I wouldn't get called on, but it didn't work. One day, I was assigned a problem at the board. I struggled through it and stood there like a flagpole. Dead silence.

Suddenly, a piece of chalk hit the chalkboard. Then another. Then another. That's how this particular teacher showed displeasure—by throwing chalk.

Next, the teacher launched into a loud lecture about stu-pidity. I was stupid for making a mistake in the problem. The class was stupid for not noticing my mistake.

Making fun of a student is rude, *rude,* RUDE. Teachers who shame kids for their mistakes should be ashamed themselves. ◆

School Manners 102: Beyond the Basics

Is not doing your homework rude, or just self-destructive? Are there cafeteria courtesies all students should know? What if you whack someone with your backpack? This chapter covers these questions and more.

Ready? Begin.

Q: Is not doing your homework rude?

A: It depends on whether this is a pattern or a one-time event. If something makes it impossible for you to finish an assignment, that's not rude at all. These things happen. Even teachers aren't always able to grade papers or prepare lessons on time because something unexpected comes up. The best thing to do is to offer an honest explanation:

> "I'm sorry, Mrs. Rousseau, but I wasn't able to do my assignment last night. There was a gas leak in our neighborhood and we had to evacuate our building. But I'll bring my paper in tomorrow."

If you're usually responsible about doing your homework, your teacher should accept your explanation.

But what if you've really fallen behind? This, too, is not necessarily rude—if you have a good reason. *Examples:* You may be feeling depressed, or your parents may have just split up, or other students may be bullying you.

Being sad, upset, or scared doesn't excuse you from doing your schoolwork. But sometimes life is too much to handle, and no matter how hard you try, you just can't cope.

Most teachers are very understanding and supportive of students who take responsibility for their actions and education. You don't have to tell a teacher personal details about your life if this makes you uncomfortable. You could say something like this:

> "I'm sorry I've gotten so far behind in my work. I'm having some problems at home, and I haven't been able to concentrate lately. I want you to know that I really like your class, and I'm trying to get caught up again."

When is it rude not to do your homework?

1. when you're lazy

2. when you're bored

3. when you're forgetful

4. when you're rebelling

5. when you're just goofing off

When some students don't live up to their part of the teacher-student bargain, this affects everyone. Class discussions slow to a crawl. Class time is spent helping students who are unprepared. Those who are prepared feel resentful. Teachers feel hurt, frustrated, and discouraged.

But the person who suffers most when you don't do your homework is *you*. Why? Because you limit your options for the future. You miss out on the pleasures and benefits of learning. You create a reputation that is unlikely to win much respect. Why be so rude to yourself?

Q: Is it bad manners to get good grades?

A: You'd think so, from the way some people behave. In some schools, kids act as if failure is cool. They tease the high-achieving students and treat them like traitors.

Let's call the high-achieving kids the HA students because, in fact, they will get the last laugh.

Why do some students badmouth others who get good grades? Because they're jealous, resentful, and hurting. Because their own insecurity makes them think that the HA students look down on them. Because the HA students' grades remind them of how poorly they're doing. Because they know, deep down, that the HA students will do things and go places in life that will be out of their reach. Dissing the HA students is a defense mechanism.

If you're a HA student and you're tired of being teased, try these ideas:

MAKE SURE THAT YOU'RE NOT SHOWING OFF OR ACTING SUPERIOR. Running through the halls shouting, "I got all A's and you didn't, you losers, loo-sers, looooooo-sers!" is not a way to win friends or keep from getting beat up.

TRY TALKING WITH THE PEOPLE WHO TEASE YOU. Ask them about their interests and activities. Congratulate them on their achievements. They may stop bothering you once they see that you're a regular person and not a stuck-up snob.

DON'T BROADCAST YOUR GRADES. If people ask how you did on a test, say, "I did fine, thanks." If they press you for the details, say, "I've decided to keep my grades private." Your friends will understand why.

And finally:

HOLD YOUR HEAD HIGH. Don't feel that you have to apologize to anyone for your intelligence, motivation, or success.

Q: Is it rude to tell teachers that you don't understand what they're talking about?

A: It *is* impolite to say, "I have no clue what you're saying. This class is a joke!" It is *not* impolite to raise your hand, wait to be called on, and ask questions when there's something you don't understand.

And don't worry about looking stupid. In fact, asking questions is a sign of intelligence. It means that you're listening and you care about learning.

Teachers know that when one student doesn't understand something, chances are neither do others. Therefore, a good teacher appreciates questions. And you'll be a hero to your classmates for having the guts to ask the same question that was going through their minds.

What if you're so confused that you don't even know what question to ask?

Raise your hand, wait to be called on, and politely say:

"Excuse me, Mr. Plato, I'm so confused that I don't even know what question to ask. Could you please explain that again?"

Mr. Plato will probably ask the class if others are confused, too. When all hands go up, he'll take another stab at the lesson. ◆

Q: Is it impolite to call someone a teacher's pet?

A: Name-calling is always boorish. However, it sometimes happens that teachers develop a special liking for certain students and let it show. These students are quickly labeled "teacher's pets."

Of course, teachers shouldn't let their personal feelings affect the way they relate to students. Good teachers try to treat all students fairly. But it's only natural that they will like some students more than others. After all, *you* like some teachers (and friends) more than others.

In most cases, students who are labeled "teacher's pets" are simply those who are interested in the subject and treat the teacher with respect. (Most teachers are turned off by brown-nosers.) If people bug you about being a teacher's pet, you might say:

"It's not my fault if Mr. Lime finds my winning personality, alert mind, and cheery attitude so attractive. I'm no different in his class than I am in Miss Lemon's, and you know she can't stand me."

If, however, you're being phony with the bologna, your classmates have a beef and the right to rib you. So, if you don't want to get lamb-basted for being a bratwurst, hold your tongue and go cold turkey with the sucking up. After all, your reputation is at steak.

7 Impressive Student Behaviors

When we asked teachers, "What manners-related behaviors most impress you in students?" these were their top 7 answers:

1. Saying "Please" and "Thank you."

2. Thoughtful listening and questioning.

3. Asking for help in a polite manner.

4. Showing kindness and understanding toward their peers and adults.

5. Free yet thoughtful expression of their views.

6. Saying they're sorry and meaning it.

7. Thanking me for teaching or helping them understand.

Q: What are the key cafeteria courtesies?

A: Throwing food. Spitting. Screeching. Chewing with your mouth open.... Wait, sorry, those are monkey-cage courtesies.

Even though school may feel like a zoo, you shouldn't look like a monkey and eat like one, too.

While good table manners are always preferable, the realities of the school environment may get in their way. ***Examples:*** If you only have 11 seconds to eat lunch and get caught up on the latest news, you may have no choice but to talk while you chew. When your menu choices are boiled hot dogs, barfaroni, and runny Jell-o, you're less likely to say, "Excuse me, Eduardo, would you mind passing the salt and pepper, please?"

Still, you can rise to the challenge and resist these downward forces. Here are some etiquette tips for feeding time:

■ Always be kind to food servers and other lunch counter personnel.

■ Don't dump anyone's tray.

■ Don't trip or tickle anyone carrying a tray.

■ Don't laugh, clap, or cheer if somebody drops a tray or glass.

■ Ask permission before you grab food off of anyone's plate. On second thought, don't grab. Allow it to be passed to you.

■ Save jokes and disgusting remarks for when your luncheon companions aren't drinking. This makes it less likely that milk will shoot out of someone's nose.

■ Throw out your trash. Don't, however, fling objects halfway across the room so they pass over others. Nobody wants your "miss" in their lap.

■ Be inclusive. It's natural to want to eat with your friends. Many schools have a tradition of "reserved" seats and tables. If someone who's not part of your circle sits down at your table, be friendly. Staring, holding your nose, making sarcastic remarks, or telling the person to get lost is rude, crude, and bad attitude, dude.

■ As you leave the cafeteria, give thanks that you don't have to wash the dishes.

SPOTLIGHT ON...
BACKPACK ATTACKS

It's important to keep guns and knives out of children's hands. But let's not forget the most dangerous weapon of all—backpacks.

The Health Information Clearinghouse for Children Using Packs (HICCUP) estimates that more people are injured each year in backpack attacks than from biking, 'boarding, and 'blading combined. Most of them were minding their own business when someone turned or pushed past them and BAM!

Most pack attackers don't mean to smack people or knock them flat. But that doesn't help their bruised and battered victims. Here's how to keep your canvas out of someone else's kisser:

- Know how much space you occupy. A small backpack or shoulder bag may add as much as a foot to your upper body depth. A large backpack with a sleeping bag, bedroll, and satellite dish may add several feet.

- Calculate your clearance before you pass fellow travelers on the road of life. If it's going to be tight, say, "Excuse me, I don't want to hit you with my pack," as you squeeze by. Even if your pack L. L. Beans them, they will be comforted by your good manners.

- If you're moving through a crowded bus, hall, or lunchroom, pretend that you're driving a car. Good drivers know exactly how much space their car occupies. This is useful information if you don't want to clobber pedestrians and clip parked cars.

- If you're running, know that your pack will be bouncing wildly to and fro. Allow extra room to pass the people in your path.

continues...

- If you're sitting down, take off your pack and tuck it under your chair. Then people won't trip over it and land in your lap, making you just another HICCUP statistic.

  What if, in spite of your best efforts, you whack someone with your pack? Stop, apologize, check for injuries, and call 911 if necessary.

Q: What is proper locker-room behavior?

A: First, it's very impolite to make snide comments about the sports equipment of others. This is a common practice among students who are forced to take showers after gym class, and it's ruuuuuuuude.

Teenage boys and girls are often sensitive about their body's development, especially when they're naked in front of 90 classmates. Perfectly normal teenagers can feel too fat or thin, short or tall, big or small.

It's important to remember that the development of secondary sex characteristics* in kids starts anywhere between ages 9 and 15. This causes great curiosity as to who's matured how far. Such interest is natural but should never cause offense. After all, it's rude to stare. Therefore, the first law of locker-room etiquette is:

---

* Secondary *whats?* In case you're wondering, secondary sex characteristics are traits that make it easier to tell the sexes apart. And they're not what you may be thinking. SSCs are not part of the reproductive system (those are the *primary* sexual characteristics). SSCs are things like breasts on females and an Adam's apple on males.

LOOK, BUT DON'T TOUCH—
AND DON'T GET CAUGHT LOOKING.

If you're shy about changing in the locker room, you can wear your gym clothes under your regular clothes. You can also protect yourself from mean-spirited classmates by sticking close to your friends. Grab lockers that are next to each other. Go as a group into the showers. And remember, the students who make the comments are usually those who are most insecure about themselves. If someone makes a rude remark about your anatomy, you can always ignore it. Or smile and say, "I wouldn't talk if I were you."

10 COMMANDMENTS
OF LOCKER-ROOM ETIQUETTE

THOU SHALT NOT...

1. hang people up by their underwear

2. snap your towel at anyone

3. run—unless you enjoy slipping and hitting your head on a bench

4. lock anyone in his or her locker

5. drip on anyone

6. hide anyone's clothes or towel

7. point, laugh, gape, or giggle at unclad classmates

8. make comments about anyone's body or body parts

9. bend over without first saying, "Excuse me, do you mind my butt in your face?"

10. bring a tape measure or magnifying glass into the showers

Q: Isn't there some manners rule against random drug testing?

A: There should be. Good manners are based on giving people the benefit of the doubt. They assume that people should be trusted until they prove not worthy. Random drug testing says, "We don't trust you. You must, on demand, prove that you're not using drugs—even if there's no visible sign that you are."

You've probably heard the standard argument for drug testing: "If you're not using drugs, you have nothing to fear." But would politicians and school board members allow hidden cameras in their homes to prove that they're not doing anything illegal?

People in favor of drug testing in schools insist that the tests are no different than sobriety tests for drivers, security checks for airline pilots, or background screenings for nuclear plant operators. But they are. Driving, flying, and working in certain fields are voluntary privileges. Practiced irresponsibly, they may put the lives of others at risk. If people object to the test, they don't have to drive, fly, or apply. Schoolchildren, however, are required by law to attend school. They can't avoid being tested by choosing to stay home.

What can you do if your school does random drug testing? Unfortunately, not much. If you refuse to be tested, you may be barred from participating in school sports or extracurricular activities. You'll have to make a choice: To pee, or not to pee?

To Cheat, or Not to Cheat?

Over the years, many students have wondered, "Is cheating bad manners?" That may seem like a reasonable question, but it ignores the main issue.

What's *right* and what's *polite* are not always the same. ***Example:*** A well-dressed gentleman walks into a bank, removes his hat, and lets a woman with two small children go ahead of him in line. Then, when he reaches the teller, he says, "Excuse me, I'm terribly sorry, but this is a robbery. Could you be so kind as to hand over the money?" His manners are perfect, but his morals are flawed.

Cheating is similar. If you use a crib sheet *and* no one notices *and* the teacher doesn't grade on a curve, cheating is not bad manners because it doesn't affect anyone but you. That does not, however, make it right. And if your cheating makes your classmates uncomfortable, or puts them at risk of getting in trouble, or changes their class standing (because your teacher *does* grade on a curve), then it definitely is bad manners. And wrong besides.

The main defense you hear for cheating is, "Everybody does it!" Everybody dies, too, but that doesn't mean we should all rush out and croak. Cheating robs you of your self-respect and self-confidence. If you cheat, chances are your friends and teachers will find out. They will think less of you for it. YOU will think less of you for it. How can you feel good about a grade you don't deserve? How can you believe in your abilities if you don't put them to a fair test? How can you be mellow if you live in fear of being caught?

If you're honest, hardworking, and passionate about something, there are a lot of routes to success besides good grades. Do the best you can without cheating. Your sense of pride and self-worth will carry you a lot further than fake A's.

When Someone Tries to Copy Off Your Paper

You're hunched over a test paper, happily filling in the little circles, when suddenly you get a creepy feeling. Your blood turns cold. The hair stands up on the back of your neck. It's almost like...*someone is watching you.*

That's because someone is. It's the same kid who always tries to copy off your paper during tests. Sometimes he's sneaky. Sometimes he's bold—especially when the teacher turns her back or leaves the room. But the results are always the same: He steals *your* answers, and you're sick of it.

What can you do? You have several choices.

CHANGE YOUR SEAT. If you can sit anywhere in the room, make sure not to sit by the cheater. If the cheater sits by you, get up and move. This may lead to a funny dance around the classroom. Sooner or later, the cheater will give up and just sit down.

What if your test-taking seat is your assigned seat? Go up to your teacher after class and ask if you can sit somewhere else in the future. If your teacher asks "Why?" and you don't want to rat on the cheater, make up another reason.

RAT ON THE CHEATER. Most schools have a strong student code against ratting and tattling. Plus many schools have very strict policies about cheating. The cheater will be punished, but you'll end up in the doghouse. So you may want to rule this out.

SEMI-RAT ON THE CHEATER. You could let your teacher know in general terms that "some people" aren't doing their own work on tests. This would probably make the teacher more watchful. But better solutions lie ahead.

COVER YOUR PAPER. This is probably the best and easiest thing to do. Shielding your answers sends a strong message to the cheater that you're not willing to let him copy from you. It also sends a message to the watchful teacher.

TALK TO THE CHEATER. Some students cheat because they're lazy or not interested in doing their schoolwork. Other students cheat because they're under great pressure to achieve. These students often feel confused, anxious, guilty, and ashamed. They feel they have no choice but to cheat.

Here's the polite way to confront someone who's copying your answers:

> "I'm sorry, but I don't let people copy my papers."

That's simple limit-setting, and it's all you need to say. It's not your job to lecture others on their morals.

But if you're feeling generous, you could add:

> "However, I would be happy to help you or explain how to do the problems later, if you're having trouble."

The cheater may tell you to take a flying leap. Or he may be touched and encouraged by your kind offer. What have you got to lose?

 **Both my friend and I are very good at math. We like doing problems, but our teacher loads on so many it's ridiculous. If ten will show that you know how to do them, she assigns a hundred. So here's what my friend and I do: She comes over to my house, I do half of the problems, she does half of the problems, and we swap answers. We almost always get them all right. Would you call that cheating?**

I would call that being efficient. ◆

Responding to Rudeness

School is so weird that it's no wonder people are rude. At no other time in your life will you have to live by a bell, store your belongings in a tiny locker, take public showers, get permission to go to the bathroom, and stand in line to eat. Unless, of course, you're sent to prison. Add to this the many daily trials of education—tests, cramped desks, strange hours, bad decorating—and rudeness is almost required.

So you're probably wondering...

If Someone's Rude to You, Is It Okay to Be Rude Back?

Here's what the teenagers we surveyed said:

YES it is	42%
NO it isn't	41%
It DEPENDS	17%

And here are some reasons they gave:

"YES, IT'S OKAY TO BE RUDE BACK BECAUSE..."

"Everyone will think you're weak if you don't."

"It's good to stand up for yourself."

"An eye for an eye."

"There's no other choice but to be rude."

In fact, there *is* another choice. But first, let's hear from some teenagers who said:

"IT DEPENDS."

"If the person is another student or peer, it's okay to be rude back. But you should never be rude to a teacher, parent, or other adult in charge."

"If someone is rude once in a while, I almost always let it go. But if a person is rude all the time, telling them off or embarrassing them will sometimes make them stop and respect me."

"It all depends on who's being rude."

Finally, let's hear from teenagers who said:

"NO, IT'S NOT OKAY TO BE RUDE BACK BECAUSE..."

"Then they'll be rude again and then you'll be rude and it'll just go in a circle."

"Why lower yourself to their childish standards?"

"You might regret it later."

"It can be a good comeback to say something positive in response to a rude comment."

What's your opinion? Do two rudes make a right? Before you decide, read on.

If you respond to rudeness with more rudeness...

- you may offend someone who didn't mean to be rude
- you may get into a fight
- you may end up in trouble yourself
- you add to the general level of rudeness in the world
- you miss the opportunity to educate or enlighten
- you let others control you—you let *them* determine how *you* will act

When you respond to rudeness with politeness...

■ you stand the best chance of stopping the behavior

■ you stand the best chance of getting what you want

■ you stand the best chance of winning others over to your cause

■ you let people know that they can't walk all over you

■ you maintain your own dignity

■ you set an example that may change the behavior of others

Rude Things Students Do (According to Teenagers)

When we asked teenagers, "What rude things do students do to each other?" these were the top 10 answers:

1. Call you names.

2. Taunt you for no reason.

3. Deliberately pass gas near you.

4. Disrespect you.

5. Talk about you behind your back.

6. Exclude you.

7. Spread rumors about you.

8. Put you down if you're different.

9. Play with your feelings.

10. Embarrass you to make themselves look good.

What's the Best Way to Respond to Rudeness?

Actually, there are *two* ways.

IGNORE IT. Let's say you're standing in the cafeteria line, waiting for your daily ration of swill. Someone barges past and almost knocks you down. He doesn't say "Excuse me." He doesn't apologize. He just keeps going.

You could yell, "You stupid idiot! Why doncha watch where you're going?" Or you could ignore it. Which is better?

If you yell, you're letting the other person pull your strings. You're being rude yourself. And you could get into an ugly argument or a fight.

If you ignore the buffoon, your arm (or whatever) will still hurt. But you'll have the satisfaction of knowing that you have good manners and self-control. And the people around you will respect you for it. They may even sympathize with you. Imagine how you'll feel when that cute guy or girl you've been dying to talk to says, "Wow, you got hit pretty hard. Are you okay?"

BE POLITE. Some people equate politeness with weakness. They think it's cool to be rude. Nothing could be further from the truth.

Politeness isn't a sign of weakness. It's a sign of *strength*. It's a powerful tool that can win you respect, protect your rights, stop rude people in their tracks, and cause adults to apologize. It can make almost any situation go your way.

If politeness is so great, you may wonder why more people don't use it. The reason is, you're not born knowing how to be polite. It's something you have to learn and practice. Not everyone is willing to make the effort. And a lot of people just don't care. But that's good for *you*. It makes your politeness stand out even more.

There are two ways to respond politely to rudeness.

Way #1: Assume that the rude person didn't really mean to be rude.

This is the secret for getting rude people to stop their behavior and/or apologize. If you accuse them of being rude, you open the door to more rudeness. If you give them the benefit of the doubt, you invite them to act differently and let them save face. ***Examples:***

ACCUSATION	INVITATION
1. You say: *"End of the line, buttface!"*	**You say:** *"Excuse me, it's kind of confusing, but the line starts back there."*
He says: *"%#@& you!"*	**He says:** *"No, excuse ME! I had no idea."*
2. You say: *"Hey, moron! You can't park there. That's a handicapped space."*	**You say:** *"I beg your pardon, the paint is so dull that you may not have noticed that's a handicapped space."*
She says: *"@%!#& you!"*	**She says:** *"Omigosh, you're right. I didn't notice. I'll move my car right away."*

About the second example: There's always the chance, however slight, that the person has a disability that isn't visible. Sometimes it's your assumption that needs correcting, not someone else's behavior.

Way #2: Instead of telling the Rude One to cut it out, ask him or her to help you out.

This strategy is based on human nature. People don't like to be scolded or told what to do. But most people are willing to change their behavior in response to a reasonable request. ***Examples:***

CUT IT OUT	HELP ME OUT
1. You say: *"Shut up! How can anyone hear what the teacher is saying when you're flapping your traps?"*	**You say:** *"Excuse me, but I have a hard time hearing Ms. Chips when she lectures. Too much loud rock-and-roll, I guess. Would you mind not talking, or at least keeping it down a bit?"*
They say: *"@%!#& you!"*	**They say:** *"Sure. Sorry, dude."*
2. You say: *"Pick up your trash, dorkhead! Do you think the hallway is your personal garbage can?"*	**You say:** *"Excuse me, but I think you dropped that soda can. If you're done with it, there's a recycling container on the other side of the hall."*
He says: *"@%!#& you!"*	**He says:** *"Oh, yeah, right. Thanks. I must have dropped it. I'll go get it."*

When people are embarrassed or their pride is hurt, they go on the defensive and lash out. When you appeal to their better nature, they get the chance to show how polite they really are.

Is it ever okay to be rude back?

Only if you don't know any better. But now you do. ◆

Getting Along with Teachers

If you follow the 30 Commandments of Classroom Etiquette on pages 9–10, and if your teachers are sane and reasonable people, then getting along with them should be a breeze. However, you may encounter difficult teachers or special circumstances as you make your way through school. Because it pays to be prepared, here's advice to keep in mind for those trying times.

What's in a Name?

One of the very first things any teacher will do is tell you his or her name, usually while writing it on the board:

"Good morning, class. My name is Mr. Baggypants.
That's B–A–Double–G–Y–P–A–N–T–S. Any questions?"

Sensitive teachers also make a point of asking any student whose name is not Jim, Bob, Pat, or Sue if they are pronouncing it right.

If your teacher doesn't do this, your best bet is to go up to him after class. This is because people, especially teachers, don't like being corrected in public.

Don't say, "You pronounced my name wrong," as this implies that your teacher made a mistake. Instead, say, "Excuse me, Mr. Baggypants," and then tell Mr. B. how you like to pronounce your name.

Be good-humored about it. There's no way a teacher will know that your parents, in their infinite wisdom, decided to name you "Karen" but pronounce it "*Cahr*-in." Or that you're French and therefore your name, Guy, rhymes with "key" and not with "sky." Or that, if you're Vietnamese, your last name is really your first name.

Your teacher will be impressed with your good manners, and you'll be off to a great start for the year.

Should I call teachers "Sir" and "Ma'am"?

Unless it's a rule at your school, you don't *have* to. But you may *want* to anyway. Here's why.

The custom of calling adults "Sir" and "Ma'am" is almost extinct in the United States. This is bad news for society but good news for you. Simply by using those two little words, you can reap huge awards with almost no effort!

Any teenager who says "Yes, Ma'am" or "No, Sir" or "Excuse me, Ma'am" (sincerely, not snidely) gets extra politeness points. These may be redeemed for many wonderful things including respect, trust, and privileges. Best of all, your sense of confidence and self-worth soars. That's what happens when you know that your behavior is admired and appreciated by others. ◆

Dealing with the Problem Teacher

The global pool of teachers, like any group of people, includes many kinds. There are saints and nurturers. Lovable eccentrics and quirky comedians. Inspiring speakers and dedicated mentors. But, by the law of averages, there are also bullies, crabapples, and nutcases with multiple personalities and delusions of grandeur. And they will, on occasion, do things that are hurtful or unfair.

Outside of school, you can usually ignore or distance yourself from people you don't like. This isn't possible in the classroom. So what do you do? You follow the Five Golden Rules for Protesting the Bad Behavior of People in Authority:

1. **Choose your moment well.** Let timing help you instead of hurt you. If you can possibly avoid it, don't approach a teacher who's in a rush or a foul mood. Wait until she has more time, patience, and warmth in her heart. Then say:

"Mrs. Moonshine, I wondered if I could please talk to you about something. Is this a good time?"

2. **Talk in private.** Nobody likes to be challenged in front of an audience. This makes them care more about scoring points and saving face than solving problems.

   If the problem must be dealt with immediately and publicly, it's even more important to follow rules 3–5.

3. **Empathize.** Teachers are human, too. A few words of understanding from a student can go a long way toward starting a fruitful discussion. Try these for openers:

   "It must be really frustrating when nobody pays attention."
   "I bet it's hard to teach when no one's done the homework."

4. **Explain, don't complain.** Accusations ("That's no fair!" "You never listen to anything anybody says!") put teachers on the defensive. If you're upset by something a teacher did, explain the situation from your point of view. Try not to mention the teacher's actions at all. *Example:* Instead of saying, "You had no right to make me take the test," say:

"I know I should have studied while I was out sick, but my headaches were so bad I couldn't read. My grade in this class is very important to me, because the only way I can go to college is if I get a scholarship."

5. **Offer alternatives.** When teachers are unjust, it's often because they're angry, hurt, frustrated, or at their wits' end. Help them. Maybe the class could hold a problem-solving session about something that's driving the teacher crazy (bullying, stealing, spitballs). Instead of counting on the teacher to come up with solutions for your situation, present your own ideas:

"Now that my headaches have gone away, I wondered if I could write an extra-credit paper on the material the test covered and try to bring up my grade."

Most teachers admire initiative. If you're not just trying to get out of doing your work, you'll be surprised by how many teachers are willing to give you a break and a fair shake.

 **Every time I get called to the board, I get nervous and embarrassed and make these stupid mistakes, and then the teacher makes fun of me in front of the whole class. I hate it!**

Boy, does *that* sound familiar. (See page 16.)

Try going up to your teacher in private. Explain that you get nervous at the board. Tell her how you feel when she makes fun of you. Suggest alternatives. ***Examples:*** Instead of doing the whole problem yourself, you could lead the class in doing it. Or maybe you could do a couple of extra problems for homework.

If, after listening, your teacher still insists that you work at the board, she may at least be more sensitive to your feelings.

The good news is: Even though you may feel humiliated and upset for days after the event, your classmates will forget about it the moment you return to your seat. They're much too worried about being called on next to focus on your errors.

If the problem persists, talk with your guidance counselor or parent. ◆

False Allegations

Teachers have a lot to do. Along with planning lessons, delivering lectures, grading papers, giving tests, and watering the bean plants on the window ledge, they must also keep order in a room full of caffeine-fueled, hormone-crazed teenagers.

If only they had eyes on the back of their head, they'd know that you weren't the one who threw the spitball, spray-painted the wall, put tacks on the cheerleaders' chairs, or stole the CDs. But they don't. Which means that sometimes they point the finger at the wrong person.

What if you get blamed for something you didn't do? And what if it happens in front of the whole class? First, take a few seconds to feel mad. That's your right. Public accusations are rude, especially when they're wrong. Then take a few deep breaths. In. Out. In. Out. In. Out. Keep deep-breathing until you calm down.

If the teacher demands an immediate response, say:

"I'm sorry, Ms. Zola, but you have the wrong person. I didn't [throw the spitball, spray-paint the wall, put tacks on the cheerleaders' chairs, steal the CDs]."

You might then experience this kind of conversation:

Ms. Z.: *"If you didn't do it, who did?"*
You: *"I don't know."*
Ms. Z.: *"Who does know?"*
You: *"I don't know."*
Ms. Z.: *"See me after class."*
You: *"Okay."*

Of course, if you *do* know who did it, you're in a pickle almost as bad as if you'd done it yourself. You'll have to choose whether to rat on the doer or keep it to yourself. By not ratting in public, you already have more politeness points than your teacher.

After class, when you meet in private, you might say something like this:

> "Ms. Z., I'm worried that a lot of people in the class will think that I did what you said I did. I'd appreciate it if you could tell the class tomorrow that I had nothing to do with it."

If a public apology is out of the question, be gracious and accept a private apology. Add up your bonus politeness points.

Blanket Punishments

No, this is not about hitting your blankie with a stick. It's about penalties that are applied to a *group* when a crime was done by *one*.

Let's say, for example, that some fool tosses an empty soda can across the room during a history quiz. The teacher doesn't see it, the doer won't admit it, and no one in the class will squeal.

So the teacher decides that you should *all* lose your study-hall privileges. Or *all* miss the field trip to the museum. Or *all* be on probation until the perpetrator confesses...no matter how long it takes.

What can you do?

First, realize that you're learning a valuable lesson: Life isn't fair. Sometimes you can do something to change that, and sometimes you can't. But it's worth a try. Approach your teacher at a calm, private moment. Don't accuse. Instead, empathize, explain, and offer an alternative:

"I'm really sorry that someone threw that can. I know it was rude and wrong. But making us all miss the field trip doesn't solve the problem, and it punishes a lot of innocent people. I really need that trip—remember I'm writing a paper on Princess Hiawatha, and there's a special exhibit about her? One of my uncles works at a hardware store. If you want, I can bring in a giant-sized trash can for the classroom. Maybe people will put their empties there. What do you think?"

This approach focuses on solving the problem rather than blaming the teacher. She just may go along with it.

 # SPOTLIGHT ON...

UNHELPFUL TEACHERS

Some teachers are always there for students. During class, before school, after school—whenever kids need help, they're available. Others act like every question or request is a burden and a nuisance.

Teachers are paid to teach. That's their job. But that doesn't relieve others from the duty of saying "Please" when they want help and "Thank you" when they get it. A teacher's willingness to help is not encouraged by students who whine, "I don't get this stupid stuff. Why do we have to learn it anyway?" Few teachers feel warmly toward students who slack off all term and then appear the day before the final demanding private instruction.

If one of your teachers seems unhelpful, it may be the fault of your school climate, not you. Try approaching her politely and respectfully. You might say:

continues...

> "Excuse me, Miss Pinchley, I'm having trouble understanding the Spanish Imposition. Is there some time when you could please help me?"

With this well-mannered query, you'll remind Miss Pinchley of why she went into teaching in the first place. You'll be a ray of sunshine and a breath of fresh air in the dark, dank swamp of her classroom.

If you ask nicely and you still get snubbed, go elsewhere. Try a classmate or another teacher. If the problem persists, talk with your mom or dad, guidance counselor, or principal.

Giving Gifts

Only one kind of "present" should be allowed in the classroom—that which follows the calling of names during roll. As in:

Teacher: *"Fred?"*
Fred: *"Present."*
Teacher: *"Ted?"*
Ted: *"Present."*
Teacher: *"Ned?"*
Ned: *"What?"*

Giving gifts to teachers places burdens on the parents (who have to pay for them), the students (who have to pick them out), and the teachers (who have to pretend they're thrilled to get them).

I speak from experience, having spent many glorious years inspiring young minds in the school environment. I witnessed the transfer of truckloads worth of perfume, scarves, and candy.

Your teachers deserve your appreciation. But if you *really* want to give a teacher a present, here are the best that money can't buy:

YOUR ATTENTION AND ENTHUSIASM THROUGHOUT THE YEAR. This is the greatest gift of all. Trust me.

A WARM LETTER OF APPRECIATION. Tell the teacher how much her teaching, example, and support have meant to you. Follow-up notes may initiate a lifelong friendship.

SUPPORT FOR BETTER SCHOOLS AND TEACHING CONDITIONS. Many schools are falling apart for lack of money. Windows are broken, walls are peeling, and there aren't enough books to go around. While teachers make pennies, people who dribble make millions.

If you want to give something back to your teachers, be an activist for higher salaries and increased funding for education. You can circulate petitions, speak at school board meetings, and encourage people to vote.

SOMETHING YOU MAKE. Take a photograph of the class and get everyone to sign it. Write a poem. Record a song you wrote. Create a work of art or craft. These are the gifts a teacher will want to keep forever.

Occasionally, a store-bought gift is fine—if it shows you made the effort to notice your teacher's interests. During the year, you can learn a lot about a teacher from what he shares with you, the way he dresses, and the physical environment of the classroom. If you discover that your teacher loves begonias, wild ties, and Tuscany, a floral print tie from Italy may be just the ticket.

Coping with Crushes

Most kids have crushes on one or more teachers before they finish school. These crushes can be based on feelings of attraction and romance, or feelings of respect and admiration. Either is normal and natural.

It's great to have a teacher you really like. It's fine to "worship" someone or to have fantasies about the person—as long as this doesn't get in the way of your schoolwork or social life. If all you can do is dream about a particular teacher, if your grades are dropping, if you're cutting yourself off from your friends, then it's not a healthy situation.

Perhaps you feel the need to be close to an adult and are projecting this onto your teacher. Are you having problems that you yearn to tell someone about? Are you and your

parents having conflicts? Your desires to be loved and listened to may fuel a crush when what you really need is someone to confide in. Talk to a school counselor, a relative, your parents, or an older sibling about your feelings. This may take some of the pressure off.

What if it seems obvious that your teacher likes you, too? He (or she) probably does...but not in *that* way. Your attentiveness, enthusiasm, and friendliness are pleasurable and rewarding to him as a teacher. But it would be a mistake to interpret his liking as romantic interest. Because he's a teacher and you're a much, much younger student, he can't have a relationship with you—no matter how much you (or he) might wish it. This would be unprofessional and illegal.

Don't tell the teacher how you feel about him. This would force him to "reject" you—which would be painful and awkward for both of you. At the end of the year, write him a thank-you note. Tell him how much you enjoyed his class and appreciated his help and interest. But don't tell him about those daydreams of you and him alone on a tropical island.

There's a teacher I can't stop thinking about. I think he likes me, too. Is it okay to give him a Valentine's Day card?

If students in your school have traditionally given cards to teachers, then yes, it's okay. If not, it's not.

If you do give a card to a favorite teacher, make sure it's not mushy or romantic. Better yet, if you give a card to one teacher, give cards to all of your teachers. ◆

Suffering Substitutes

What is it about a substitute teacher that brings out the worst in students? Why does a normally well-behaved class turn into a pack of spitball-lobbing rowdies when the "real teacher" is away? For what reason do otherwise polite students delight in tormenting temps?

Who knows? And who cares? This book isn't about reasons. It's about manners. And it's impolite to make subs squirm—or, as has happened on more than one occasion, burst into tears and flee the room.

Substitute teachers enter the classroom at a disadvantage. They come on short notice, don't know the students, are unfamiliar with the teacher's rituals, and may never see the class again. They lack the teaching tools and clout that

BUT OUR REGULAR TEACHER LETS US DO THIS

come from having history with, personal relationships with, and future report cards for the students. To take advantage of this is the height of rudeness. It is like (and I mean no disrespect) torturing a turtle on its back.

While it may be common practice in your school to give subs a hard time, that doesn't make it right. The presence of a substitute presents you with a rare opportunity to reap the rewards of good manners. This is because the behavior of the class reflects upon the absent teacher. Being helpful and polite not only makes the sub feel welcome and respected. It also makes her think highly of your teacher. So when the sub leaves her report (which all subs do), it will be full of praise for those students who made her stay so pleasant.

Is it okay to totally ignore a sub and do whatever I want?

Only if your sub is a sandwich. ◆

How to Dress for School Success

Each day, when you wander to your closet, dresser, or Everest-size heap of clothes on the floor, you're not just deciding what to wear. You're deciding what you want to tell the world about yourself. When you walk out the door, your clothes will say:

"I'm cool."	*or*	"I'm trying to be cool."
"I care about how I look."	*or*	"I'm a slob."
"I spend a lot on clothes."	*or*	"I shop at thrift stores."
"I want to be noticed."	*or*	"I want to blend in."

"I'm trying to look older."	*or*	"I'm trying to look younger."
"I respect social traditions."	*or*	"I couldn't care less about society."

Of course, your clothes might also say:

University of Delaware

Abercrombie & Fitch

The Hives

My parents went to Tobago and all I got was this lousy T-shirt

Clothes can tell you whether someone is a police officer, Girl Scout, aging hippie, soldier, flight attendant, nurse, convict, businessperson, or baseball player. And because clothes make such powerful statements, the way you dress can be a source of conflict at school.

Let's look at some of the issues involved.

Why Clothes Matter

Why does everybody make such a big deal about clothes? As long as you're not going around naked, why does it matter what you wear?

It matters because clothes are symbolic. They make a statement about your attitudes, status, and self-image, even if that's not what you intend.

When you say that you "like" certain clothes, what do you like about them? Probably the way they make you look and feel. Whether you're aware of it or not, you're drawn to the associations those clothes trigger in your mind:

"I'm hip."

"I'm hot."

"I'm artistic."

"I'm bad."

"I'm laid back."

"I'm politically correct."

"I'm totally uninterested in clothes, which is why I decided to wear these particular clothes—because they show how uninterested I am. It took me hours to pick them out and get them to look just right."

There's no way to avoid being judged by what you wear. Before the first word pops out of your mouth, your clothes and appearance have already said a lot about you. The problem is, what it says may not be true. ***Example:*** You could shave your head, get a swastika tattoo, put on boots and camouflage gear, and the world would think you're a neo-Nazi skinhead. You'd still be your same sweet self, but your image would say otherwise—and people would react accordingly.

This is why the first thing a defense attorney does is a client makeover. The serial murderer who, when arrested, looked like a cross between Bigfoot and the Big Bad Wolf will enter the courtroom looking like Santa Claus on his way to church.

School Dress Codes

It's ironic. It's frustrating. It's totally unfair. At a time when clothes are a main way of expressing yourself, adults tell you what to wear!

Maybe your parents have banned certain clothes, makeup, or hairstyles. Fine. You can always sneak your midriff top, low-rise pants, and mascara into your backpack before leaving for school, then change in the bathroom when you get there.

Unless, of course, your school has a dress code. Which many schools do, and their numbers are growing.

Your school may have a strict dress code that spells out what you can and can't wear from head to toe. You may even be required to wear a school uniform (see pages 65–66 for more on that topic). Or you may have the right to dress however you like in school, with certain restrictions: no halter tops, no body piercings, no T-shirts with "%#@&!" printed on them.

You may think that restrictions are reasonable. Or you may think they're oppressive. You may go along with them; after all, you won't be in school forever. Or you may conclude that they limit your right to free speech, and that's something you can't live with.

If you defy them, people will make judgments accordingly. And there may be consequences. You may be asked to change clothes or turn your T-shirt inside-out. Your parents might be called. There may be in-school suspension, out-of-school suspension, or legal action.

It's up to you to decide whether what you wear will hurt you or help you. Is an anarchy T-shirt worth getting suspended for? Are multiple facial piercings worth getting kicked off the swim team? If they are, go for it. Just make sure the battles are worth the wounds.

Before you fight your school's dress code, talk with your dad or mom. Talk with a teacher or another adult you trust and respect. Consider the possible consequences. What might you lose? What might you win? Believe it or not, you may look back later in life and wonder what all the fuss was about.

SPOTLIGHT ON...
WHAT NOT TO WEAR

Here are just some of the things that school dress codes forbid students to wear in school or at school-sponsored events:

- Hats, caps, bandannas, beanies, or head coverings of any kind, except for religious or medical reasons

- Shirts or other clothing with logos, political slogans, racial or ethnic slurs or symbols, gang symbols, profanity, offensive language, or subversive language

- Clothing or jewelry that advertises alcohol, drugs, or tobacco

- Clothing or jewelry that promotes gang, cult, or racist activity

- Clothing or accessories that are sexually suggestive or inflammatory

- Clothing that exposes the midriff, back, or shoulders

- Clothing that is low-cut, high-cut, tight, transparent, ripped, or torn

- Visible undergarments

- Jewelry, body art, and piercings deemed "dangerous" or "distracting"

- Pajama pants, lounge pants, or cargo pants

- Excessively saggy or baggy pants

- Skirts, shorts, or skorts shorter than knee-length

- Long coats or jackets

- Open-toed shoes, flip-flops, beach shoes, platform shoes, high-heeled shoes

- Sunglasses when inside the building

- Exotic makeup or hair dye

- Large, long, and/or heavy chains

- Anything that would "create an unsafe situation in any class"

- Anything that "detracts in any way from the educational mission of the school's instructional program"

School Uniforms

Should teenagers be required to wear uniforms in school? It depends on who you ask.

Some school authorities have decided that the only thing wrong with our educational system is the way kids dress. So, instead of dealing with crumbling buildings, overworked teachers, and scarce resources, they send parents and kids out to buy white shirts and navy pants.

Supporters of school uniforms claim that academic performance increases, and disciplinary problems decrease, when schools make kids dress alike. This may be true. *But it's not because of the uniforms.* It's because schools that require them are likely to be schools where teachers and administrators respect students and expect them to behave responsibly. They are schools where parents are involved in their children's education, where conflict resolution and peer mediation programs are in place, and where community values are clearly stated and fairly enforced.

In short, they are schools where the climate is based on the highest principles of good manners. If you took away the khaki pants, those schools would function just as well (although kids might complain about their legs being cold).

Teens against school uniforms claim that they infringe upon their rights to life, liberty, and the pursuit of designer labels. What some of these clothes-minded teens don't get is that freedom of dress, like other freedoms, must be exercised responsibly. The role of fashion in determining school status can be so extreme that kids spend more time each day choosing outfits than doing homework. Families that can barely put food on their table buy $150 sneakers so their teen won't be a social outcast.

When clothing is used to show disrespect, promote snobbery, exclude, and embarrass, this is not well-mannered. Nor does it help to create a positive school climate.

Ultimately, school uniforms are about politics and power, not etiquette. If students don't want to be dressed alike, they should stop fighting each other over their clothes and stop judging each other by the price of their jeans. And if school authorities want to do a makeover, they should do it on the school, not the students.

Meanwhile, if your school requires a uniform, you'll have to grin and wear it.

SPOTLIGHT ON...
DETAILS, DETAILS

Uniform or not, the latest fashion or hand-me downs—it won't matter what you wear if your face is dirty, your hair is greasy, your nails are grungy, and you stink.

We're talking hygiene. Except that word sounds so...sanitary. So let's come up with a new way to say it: *self-detailing*. Surely you deserve as much care as the family car. Before you set off for the day, pull in for a pit stop and run through your checklist:

- ❑ BODY: Washed? Sweet-smelling?

- ❑ FACE: Scrubbed? Shaved? Made-up?

- ❑ HAIR: Cleaned? Conditioned? Combed?

- ❑ TEETH: Brushed? Flossed? De-bugged?

- ❑ FINGERNAILS: Trimmed? Filed? Painted? Polished?

- ❑ NOSTRILS: Emptied?

- ❑ EARS: De-waxed?

- ❑ SKIN: Oiled? Lotioned? Perfumed? Sunblocked? Stridexed?

- ❑ CLOTHES: Laundered? Ironed? Right-side out? Reasonably well-fitting?

If you treat yourself to this sort of daily detailing, you'll run better, last longer, and turn heads when you drive, er, walk by.

Hats in School

Many schools are banning baseball caps inside the building. Your school might be among them. Some students are asking, "Does this violate our rights? Should we take the school board to court?" These students are missing the point. This isn't a legal issue. It's an etiquette issue.

Baseball caps are grand. They're handy, jaunty, and, when worn with the visor to the rear, they make you look like your head's on backwards. Personally, I'm all for them—just not in school.

Why not? *Because etiquette demands that gentlemen remove their hats when they are indoors.* This makes sense. Hats were designed to:

1. keep your head warm
2. protect you from sun and precipitation
3. keep your hair from blowing all over creation, and
4. hide baldness

Since you're not yet bald (unless you shave your head), your only reason to wear a hat would be to protect you from the elements. Unless your school has no roof, you don't really need to wear a hat in the classroom.

Your school may have more reasons for not wanting students to wear hats indoors. For one thing, a hat prevents teachers from seeing your eager little face. It's not very rewarding to teach a class of visors. Caps also make it hard for teachers to identify students when they raise their hands. Who should they call on first? Nike, North Face, John Deere, or Diesel?

Your school may also be concerned about gang warfare. The color or tilt of a cap can be used to identify oneself as a member of a particular gang, or to challenge someone in another gang. Wear the wrong cap and you could end up getting beaten or worse. This disrupts the educational process. If nobody is allowed to wear caps, it eliminates the problem—at least within the school building.

The final reason for banning baseball caps in schools is a practical one: As your head fills with knowledge, it must have room to expand.

Do you see anything wrong with boys wearing an earring?

I see nothing wrong with boys wearing a small, modest earring—one that doesn't look like an Alexander Calder mobile. In fact, I've often thought it unfair that women can adorn themselves with any number of rings, necklaces, baubles, pearls, diamonds, earrings, and brooches while men must make do with a lousy tie tack. ◆

Bullies, Bigots, Bashers, and Harassers

It's tough enough sitting on hard chairs while teachers drone on and on. It's bad enough dealing with the cliques and groups that are part of every school's social climate. Add in the bullies, bigots, gay-bashers, and sexual harassers, and school is almost too much to bear.

You can ignore their bad behavior. Or you can shine like the fine human being you are and do something about it.

Busting Bullies

You've seen students at your school getting picked on, and you're sick of it. Bullying pollutes your school climate. Not only is it rude, it's harmful and potentially deadly. Some bullying victims have dropped out of school. Some have committed suicide.

If you witness an act of bullying, don't just stand there. Try one or more of these ideas:

SUPPORT AND COUNSEL THE VICTIM. Say:

> "Don't let what Fowler says get to you. Everybody knows he's a jerk."

> "He's just doing it because you get so angry. Stay calm, hang out with us for a while, and try not to show that it bothers you."

CONFRONT THE BULLY IN PRIVATE. Take him aside and say:

> "Look, Fowler, you probably don't realize this, but Chumpley doesn't like being teased. I'm only telling you because I know you're not the sort of person who'd hurt someone on purpose."

Of course, this is a total crock. And that's what makes good manners so much fun. Fowler may be so stunned by your appeal to his better nature that he'll lighten up on Chumpley.

CONFRONT THE BULLY IN PUBLIC. Many bullies count on bystanders doing nothing or pretending not to notice. If you see someone being hassled in the hall or bullied on the bus, speak up. Say:

"Cut it out. Nobody thinks you're funny or cool."
"Leave him alone. How'd you like to be treated that way?"

ENLIST THE SUPPORT OF BYSTANDERS. Turn to the people around you and say:

"Does anyone else hate it when Fowler picks on people?"

Chances are good that others feel the same way you do. Following your example, they will say something, too.

APPEAL TO HIGHER AUTHORITIES. In the past, bullies called names, stole lunches, and bloodied noses. Today's bullies may be packing AK-47s. This is no joke. "Normal" school-yard hazing now includes extortion, emotional terrorizing, and drive-by shootings.

It used to be believed that bullies were sad, lonely, insecure children who used fear and aggression to gain attention and status. Recent research suggests that many bullies have tons of friends and self-confidence. They're not hurting at all. They've simply learned (from movies, TV, friends, and family) that violence and intimidation can get them what they want.

If these are the bullies in your school, it may be dangerous for you to confront them directly. Instead, talk to your parents, guidance counselor, school authorities, or the police. You shouldn't have to enter a war zone to get an education.

Besting Bigots

You've heard the comments, the sneers, and the slurs, and you've decided that enough is enough. Time for action! The key to besting bigots is refusing to tolerate their tasteless remarks.

How you respond will depend on the circumstances. Start by considering the source of the insult. Some bigoted comments are unintentional. The speaker isn't really prejudiced, just clueless. This doesn't make the comment any less ugly. But it does give you the chance to educate the speaker.

Example: Your five-year-old brother calls someone a "fag." Since little kids often repeat words they hear, ask your brother if he knows what the word means. If he doesn't, tell him. Because he's so young, you'll have to choose your words to fit his level of understanding. You could say something like this:

> "You know how Mom and Dad live and sleep together? Well, some grown-ups prefer to live and sleep with people of the same sex. Men who do this are called 'gay' or 'homosexual.' 'Fag' is a nasty word for a gay man. We don't use that word in our family because it's mean and hurtful."

Or: An exchange student struggling to learn English makes a comment about the "colored" students in your school. Explain to her that the word "colored" is offensive to many people because of its historical associations. Suggest that she use "black" or "African American" instead.

Or: Your grandfather, who lives with you, calls your female classmates "honey" when they come to visit. Since he means to be gracious, not sexist, your job is to fill him in on the social changes of the past few decades. Tell him that young ladies of today don't appreciate being called "honey," no matter how sweet they are. Suggest that he refer to your friends by their given names.

Unfortunately, most bigoted comments aren't accidental or innocent. They are the result of fear, ignorance, and/or prejudice. Silence suggests approval, and it doesn't stop hatred. As the 18th-century English statesman Edmund Burke once said, "The only thing necessary for the triumph of evil is for good men to do nothing."*

---

*If Burke had been a 21st-century statesperson, he would have said "good men and women."

It's easy to do nothing about bigotry in school. There's a lot of pressure to fit in and go along with the crowd. Deep down, you know it's wrong, but no one else is doing anything, so why should *you* be the one to stick your neck out?

Because if you're not part of the solution, you're part of the problem.

If you take a stand, the bigots may respond, "You say we should be tolerant. Well, where's *your* tolerance for *our* beliefs?" Don't be taken in by this bogus "defense." Tolerate intolerance the same way you do air pollution: Accept that it exists, recognize it as bad, and do everything in your power to eliminate it.

If you speak out against bigotry, the worst that can happen is you'll be disliked, scorned, or snubbed by people whose behavior is cruel, ignorant, offensive, hateful, and/or illegal. Like, big loss. The best that can happen is you'll find that most of your classmates feel the same way you do. Once you break the ice, they'll cheer your courage and support your cause. You'll be a leader in creating a friendly, respectful, and inclusive climate for your school.

Following are five ways to respond to bigoted jokes and comments. Bigotry is not an excuse for being rude back. In fact, politeness is the most powerful weapon you can use.

1. **Walk out.** You may attend a lecture or performance in which the speaker (or comedian, or musician) makes bigoted remarks. It may be impolite or impractical to speak out at the time. There may not be a chance for you to challenge the remarks in a question-and-answer session or discussion. Therefore, get up and leave. Do it quietly. Don't disturb others. Your statement will be seen and "heard." Others may follow your example.

2. **Stare.** We all know that it's rude to stare. So let's rephrase this: "Take an intense visual focus." Aiming laser looks at someone who makes an offensive remark is a powerful way to show disapproval. Especially if others follow your lead. The target of 12 pairs of humorless eyes is likely to squirm, sweat, and wonder if he said something wrong.

3. **Question the speaker.** Many bigots assume that everyone present shares their view. Therefore, it can be quite unsettling if you draw attention to their remark by asking about it. *Example:* Someone makes a racist comment. With a pleasant expression and tone, you could say:

"Excuse me?"
 "I beg your pardon?"
"I'm sorry, I must have misheard you."

If the person repeats the offensive remark, you can repeat what you just said:

"I'm sorry, I STILL think I must have misheard you."

This is a bit like the parent who says, "I can't hear you!" over and over until a child gets a clue and says, "Please."

4. **Ask for an explanation.** In the face of a bigoted comment or joke, say:

"I'm sorry, I don't get it. Could you please explain the joke to me?"

It's a perfectly civilized question, but the spotlight it shines on the speaker and the remark is stunning. You could also ask:

"Do you think that's funny?"

5. **Reveal a connection.** Another way to respond to bigotry is to let the speaker know that you have a personal stake in the matter:

"You may not realize that my mother is Polish."
"Actually, my stepfather is a Muslim."
"I'm sure you're unaware that my older brother is gay."

The speaker may fall all over herself with an apology and say that she didn't mean anything disrespectful and some of her best friends are Polish or Muslim or gay, if not all three. Or she may accuse you of not being able to "take a joke."

You challenge discrimination, intolerance, and hatred because it's the right thing to do. Don't expect to change a bigot's mind. If that happens, great. If it doesn't, at least the person might shut up and keep his ideas to himself. But no matter what happens, you'll feel proud. Plus your actions will have a powerful effect on those who witness them. Because of you, they may speak out in the future.

What's so bad about ethnic jokes? They're funny.

Which are the funny ones? Those about your ethnicity or someone else's?

Ethnic jokes are like getting your pants pulled down in school. If it happens to someone else, it's humorous. If it happens to you, it's hurtful.

Don't get me wrong; some ethnic jokes are very funny. And we all need to lighten up before political correctness turns humor into an endangered species. Poking fun at a group of people isn't always disrespectful. Many jokes that do this are good-natured; they tease, but without being malicious. But other jokes are rooted in prejudice. They are mean-spirited and reinforce the stereotypes that feed bigotry.

I'm not suggesting that you stick to knock-knock jokes for the rest of your life. But before you tell a joke, ask yourself, "Would I be comfortable if people associated this joke with me?" By "people," I don't just mean your closest friends and locker-room buddies. I mean your mom and dad, maybe your priest or pastor or rabbi, maybe the family of another race who lives across the hall from you, maybe the kid you know who's in a wheelchair, maybe the kid who's gay but hasn't yet come out. Would *they* think the joke is funny? ◆

Blocking Gay Bashers

Homophobia—the irrational fear of homosexuals—breeds discrimination, violence, and hate. It also causes the depression and isolation that leads many gay and lesbian teens to abuse drugs and commit suicide.

Persecution of gay, lesbian, bisexual, and transgender (GLBT) people is so common that there's even a special name for it: gay bashing. Most teens who are gay, "look gay," or "act gay" will never, thankfully, be seriously assaulted—or worse. But they are likely to be taunted, threatened, or harassed.

Gay bashing is R-U-D-E. No school should tolerate it. On a personal level, *you* shouldn't tolerate it. Whether you're straight, gay, or not yet sure (a lot of teens question their sexual orientation and/or gender identity), you can take positive action. Start with these ideas:

IF PEOPLE CALL YOU GAY: Don't respond, "I am not!" First, your sexuality isn't anyone's business but yours. Second, being defensive plays into their hands. It also suggests that there's something wrong with being gay. So just ignore them or calmly say:

> "You seem very interested in other people's sexuality. Do you have some questions or concerns about your own that you'd like to share with me?"

IF PEOPLE MAKE JOKES ABOUT BEING GAY: Look back at the five ways to respond to bigoted jokes and comments on pages 77–79. You might also say:

> "You know, I really don't like jokes that make fun of gay people."

If someone responds, "Why, are YOU gay?" you can say:

> "You don't have to be gay to think those jokes are lame."

IF YOU KNOW SOMEONE WHO'S BEING TEASED OR HARASSED: Be a friend. Offer your support. Tell the person that you'll stand by him or her. Then walk the talk. Hang out together. Do things together. Be seen together at school, at the mall, and in other places where kids gather.

IF YOU WITNESS OR HEAR ABOUT A THREAT OR VIOLENCE:
Report it right away. Don't mess around. Tell a teacher,
counselor, or the principal.

**IF YOUR SCHOOL DOESN'T HAVE A SUPPORT GROUP FOR GLBT
TEENS:** Approach school authorities about starting one.
TIP: Many straight kids join such groups as a way to express
their solidarity.

10 Myths and 11 Facts About Gay People

1. **Myth:** HIV/AIDS is spread by gay people.
   Fact: HIV/AIDS is spread by behavior, not sexual orientation.
   Today it's spreading much faster among straights than gays.

2. **Myth:** Gay people only care about sex.
   Fact: Gay people are just as interested in long-term,
   committed relationships as straight people. Otherwise, why
   would they care about gay marriage?

3. **Myth:** People choose to be gay.
   Fact: Sexual orientation isn't something people choose.
   It's something they discover about themselves.

4. **Myth:** Most child molesters are gay.
   Fact: More than 90 percent of child molesters are straight.

5. **Myth:** Being gay means you're sick or perverted.
   Fact: Neither the medical nor psychiatric professionals view
   homosexuality as a sickness or perversion.

6. **Myth:** If you're gay, you can be cured.
   Fact: Since homosexuality isn't a sickness, there's nothing
   to "cure."

7. **Myth:** Having a crush on, fantasy about, or sexual experience
   with someone of the same sex means you're gay.
   Fact: Most straight adults have had one or all of these
   experiences while growing up.

8. **Myth:** Gays try to recruit kids into being gay.
   Fact: No one can be "recruited" to be gay—or straight.

9. **Myth:** Gays and lesbians aren't fit to be parents.
   Fact: Gay and lesbian parents are just as capable of raising
   healthy, happy children as straight parents are.
   Bonus Fact: Children raised by gay or lesbian parents are
   no more likely to grow up gay or lesbian than other children.

10. **Myth:** I don't know any gay people.
    Fact: You probably do. You just don't realize it yet.

Stopping Sexual Harassment

Sexual harassment is rude and crude. It's also illegal. It is not
a sign of affection, and it is not a compliment. At its *least*
offensive, sexual harassment is insensitive, annoying, and
clumsy. At its *most* offensive, it's hostile, scary, and violent.

While most victims of sexual harassment are girls, it
happens to boys, too. Here are some examples of sexually
harassing behaviors that have been reported in U.S. high
schools:

- unwanted touching

- comments about a person's looks, parts of the body, or
  what type of sex the person would be "good at"

- name-calling
- spreading sexual rumors
- leers, stares
- telling sexual or dirty jokes
- displaying pornography or sexually oriented cartoons or pictures
- pressuring someone for sexual activity
- cornering, blocking, or standing too close to someone
- publicly "rating" an individual (like on a scale from 1–10)
- giving snuggies or wedgies
- sexual assault or attempted sexual assault
- rape
- touching or exposing oneself sexually in front of others

- sexual graffiti
- making kissing, smacking, or sucking sounds
- catcalls, whistles
- repeatedly asking someone out when she or he isn't interested
- pulling down someone's pants or skirt
- suggestive facial expressions (winking, kissing)
- "slam books" (lists of students with sexual comments written about them by other students)

You might be questioning some of the items on this list. In fact, you might be asking yourself, "What's wrong with a friendly touch, comment, or whistle? Is flirting a crime?" And even, "Can't a person have fun anymore?"

Of course you can have fun—just not at someone else's expense. Maybe you don't mean to harass someone with your interest and/or affections. But sexual harassment is defined by the person on the *receiving* end, not the *giving* end.

If your actions or words cause someone to feel embarrassed, humiliated, afraid, powerless, invaded, or degraded, it's sexual harassment, not flirting. If the person asked or signaled you to stop and you didn't, it's sexual harassment, not flirting.

FLIRTING...	**SEXUAL HARASSMENT...**
...makes people feel valued, flattered, attractive, and respected	...makes them feel confused, angry, intimidated, and demeaned
...boosts self-esteem	...damages self-esteem
...is two-sided	...is one-sided
...is wanted	...is unwanted

During adolescence, you have a lot of new sexual feelings and start to want deeper relationships with people. As you explore these new relationships, you may feel awkward or confused. You may not be sure if someone likes you, or how they like you. You may wonder:

"Is it okay to put my arm around her waist?"

"Is it okay to give him a good-night kiss?"

"Is it okay to compliment her on what she's wearing?"
"Is it okay to tell him he turns me on?"

The answers to these questions aren't always clear. Human love and sexual desire are among the most powerful and mysterious feelings we have. There's no way to regulate flirting or dating to guarantee that no one will ever get hurt or be misunderstood. And it would be a tragedy if schools, in their efforts to eliminate harassment, also eliminated warmth, trust, and affection between students.

As long as you practice courtesy in your relationships, you probably don't need to worry about overstepping the bounds of flirting. Stay alert for verbal and physical cues. Take things slowly. Ask permission. Say, "May I...?" "Do you mind if...?" "Is this all right with you?"

Another way to monitor your behavior and remarks is to ask yourself these questions:

1. "Would I mind if somebody else did or said this to my sister, mother, or girlfriend (or brother, father, or boyfriend)?"

2. "Would I mind if a video of my behavior were shown to my parents, friends, teachers, and/or classmates?"

Obviously, you might be doing something perfectly acceptable and mutually desired which, for reasons of privacy, you'd rather not see at your neighborhood multiplex. What we're talking about here is stuff that you'd be ashamed of—stuff that would reflect poorly on your character or reputation.

If you make a real effort to be sensitive to the needs and feelings of others, you won't be considered a sexual harasser. But you might be considered very sexy.

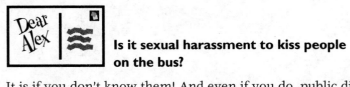

Is it sexual harassment to kiss people on the bus?

It is if you don't know them! And even if you do, public displays of affection can make others uncomfortable. Why risk a fuss about a buss? You'll make out better if you wait until you get off. ◆

Civility
at Sporting Events

Whether you're watching or participating, it pays to be polite at school sporting events. That way, you get to stay until the end.

Spectator Etiquette

If you go to a school concert, it's rude to yell, "Kill the bassoonist!" If you go to a school play, it's ill-mannered to chant, "We want an actor, not a weed whacker!"

The standards are more relaxed at school sporting events. It's acceptable to insult game officials and opposing team members. However, these insults must be related to the target's athletic role, performance, and/or relevant body parts. In other words, the eyes of an umpire, the arms of a pitcher, and the I.Q. of a coach are all fair game. The umpire's mother, the pitcher's religion, and the coach's race are not.

But just because tradition allows verbal abuse from the stands doesn't mean it's a good thing. What if, instead, we heap praise and hurrays on our own team? At a time when too few people practice even the basics of politeness, do we need to make rudeness a normal part of sporting events? This only encourages those who would spit on umpires or throw iceballs from the stands.

Look at World Cup soccer. It has been overrun by hooligans out to hit someone over the head with a bottle of beer. And the fans are even worse!

It's time to rethink spectator behavior at sporting events. A bit more "Well played, sir!" and a bit less "Throw the bum out!" can do no harm. After all, teams should be uplifted by their athletic supporters.

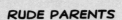

SPOTLIGHT ON...
RUDE PARENTS

Some of the worst offenders in school sports aren't the kids in the stands. They're the parents of the players. They scream at the coaches. They shout at the umpires. They hurl insults at the players, including their own kids. Parents have even been known to get into fistfights with each other.

If this is a problem at your school's sporting events, talk to the coaches. They can speak to particular parents or send a letter home to all parents, reminding them of the importance of good sportsmanship. During games, they can also go up to offending parents and tell them to nix the nasty remarks.

Meanwhile, parents who behave badly should have to sit in the corner and go to bed without supper.

Player Etiquette

Sports etiquette is the ultimate test of good manners. This is because good sportsmanship sometimes requires you to act the opposite of how you're feeling. *Example:* You've had your face wiped in the mud all afternoon, lost by one fluky goal in the last two seconds of play, and been knocked out of the finals. It's hard, so very hard, to hold out your hand to the winners and say, "Great game!" What you really feel like saying is, "You lucky shmucks!" Or something like that.

Why must you put your feelings aside? Because "It's not whether you win or lose, it's how you play the game."

Yeah, right. If you believe that, I've got another one for you: "Sticks and stones may break your bones, but names will never hurt you."

Of course it matters whether you win or lose! Duh! Self-confidence, scholarships, career paths, and endorsements can all be affected by your win-lose stats. But it's your behavior before, during, and after every match that determines whether, as a human being, you're a winner or a loser. You can be a winning athlete but a loser in life. And you can be a losing athlete but a winning person.

Here's how to be a winner, no matter how the game turns out:

HAVE FUN. What's the point of being out there if you're not enjoying yourself? Good vibes are contagious. Your teammates will catch your enthusiasm and the game will be that much more enjoyable for all.

AVOID TEMPER TANTRUMS. Nobody wants to witness an immature outburst. Resist the impulse to throw your tennis racquet, hit ballboys or ballgirls, curse at umpires, or storm off the court. Only professional players making millions of dollars are allowed to do these things.

DON'T MAKE EXCUSES. If you mess up, say you're sorry and let it go. You only draw more attention to yourself if you blame the sun, the wind, the ref, the racquet, or the gopher hole. If it truly wasn't your fault, that will be obvious to everyone.

DON'T BLAME OTHERS. If your team members mess up, give them encouragement, not criticism. Saying, "Good try," or, "Don't worry," will do a lot more to help than, "Smooth move, Ex-Lax."

CONGRATULATE THE WINNERS. This is how character is built. Hold out your hand and tell the victors they played a great game.

COMPLIMENT THE LOSERS. But be sincere. Don't tell them they played well when it's obvious they didn't. Instead, you might say:

> "I really enjoyed the game."
>
> "Thanks for playing us."
>
> "You guys had an off day today, but you were great against Lincoln last week."

CHOOSE UP SIDES WITH TACT. It feels terrible, time after time, to be the last person chosen for a team. You stand there, staring at your sneakers, hoping that the next pick will put you out of your misery. Finally, everyone's been chosen except you and somebody says, "Ha, ha. You get Waskow." This is the stuff of which lifetime traumas are made.

Many gym teachers now form teams randomly by counting off by twos or fours. If you're one of the captains choosing up sides, strike a blow for kindness. Tell the other captain (discreetly) to pick people in *reverse* order. Start with the *worst* players. Of course, everyone will know what you're doing. But the kids usually picked last will worship you for life. And the star athletes will get a useful lesson in humility as they experience what it feels like to stand in the dwindling line as everyone else high-fives their way onto the team.

A few final suggestions for politeness on the playing field:

■ If you mistakenly kick the goalie's head instead of the ball, say, "Excuse me."

■ If you tackle someone, upon removing your cleats from his groin and your fingers from his eyeballs, it's a nice gesture to help him up.

■ In basketball, don't pull down anyone's shorts as he or she goes up for a jump shot.

Applying to Colleges

One day before too long, many of you will start applying to colleges.* Most colleges require applicants to write an essay describing their interests, goals, and/or reasons for wanting to go there. Some ask prospective students to tell about an experience from which they learned something.

If you find yourself facing the second type of essay question, you may wonder how truthful to be. Or is this a case where honesty maybe isn't the best policy?

In fact, there are times when the truth, the whole truth, and nothing but the truth could lead to that Great Rejection

---

*Or other secondary-type, continuing-education schools. No matter where you want to go, you'll have to convince someone to let you in. So even if you're not applying to Harvard or Yale, pay attention to these useful tips for presenting yourself as the kind of learner who will make any institution proud.

Pile in the Sky. Telling a college that your major interests are sex and getting away from home is not the way to win the heart and mind of an admissions officer.

The key to applying to college is the key to life: *Balance*.

■ You want to say what they want to hear without sounding phony.

■ You want your application to stand out without being showy.

■ You want to reveal your achievements without appearing boastful.

■ You want to show that you have the motivation to be successful without seeming money-grubbing.

In short, you want to present yourself as:

creative	*without being*	flaky
cooperative	*without being*	spineless
independent	*without being*	rebellious
confident	*without being*	cocky
principled	*without being*	intolerant
enthusiastic	*without being*	ditsy
well-rounded	*without being*	unfocused
socially aware	*but not*	self-righteous

Or, to put it simply: Applying to college involves everything you've learned (and are learning) about good manners. Just present yourself as a sincere, tolerant, observant, secure individual who, while marching to your own drumbeat, is aware of other people's rights and sensibilities.

Tips for Well-Mannered Applications and Interviews

REMEMBER THAT THE PURPOSE OF FILLING OUT AN APPLICATION IS TO GET INTO THAT SCHOOL. It is not to write an autobiography titled *Confessions of a Young Punk*. If you include anything that might raise eyebrows, describe it as a profound learning experience. Explain how you've grown as a result.

DRESS APPROPRIATELY. Admissions officials have no interest in seeing the top six inches of your underwear or the bottom six inches of your cleavage. Wear something casual enough to feel comfortable, and dressy enough to show that you respect the occasion and have made an effort.

BE ON YOUR BEST BEHAVIOR. This is the time to pull out all the manners stops. Stand up when the interviewer comes to greet you. Offer a firm handshake. Look 'em in the eye. Use "Sir" and "Ma'am." Sit up straight. Try not to fidget. When the interview ends, thank the admissions official and say that you enjoyed talking.

SHOW ENTHUSIASM. It's not a good sign if your interviewer falls asleep in the middle of your interview. Don't be a lifeless lump. Speak up. Put a sparkle in your eyes. Don't mumble. Convey the kind of energy you will apply to your studies. No, on second thought, better not.

DEMONSTRATE KNOWLEDGE OF THE INSTITUTION. Show that you've at least read the catalog. It would be embarrassing to blab about your passion for architecture, and then learn that the college doesn't have a design school.

COME WITH QUESTIONS. It never hurts to have a few intelligent questions ready in case the interviewer asks if you have any. You can inquire about the curriculum, cultural life, volunteer programs, academic policies, sports requirements, social opportunities, and so on. Try not to ask anything that would be obvious to anyone who'd done her homework (like, "How many years does it take to get a degree?").

There are several fictions to the application process that both sides agree not to examine too closely. For example, applicants pretend that all of their extracurricular activities were motivated by the love of learning and the desire to help others, not by the craving to get into college. They also pretend that the college they are currently considering is their first choice.

Meanwhile, colleges pretend that the decisions they make are objective. Big surprise—they aren't. Most students are fully qualified to attend the schools they apply to. *Example:* Which student will get accepted? The one with straight A's who loves history, heads the lacrosse team, plays flute, and works with the homeless? Or the one with straight A's who loves math, heads the tennis team, plays guitar, and works with inner-city youth? The ultimate decision could go either way. And it probably will depend on how the tennis and lacrosse teams have been doing. For this reason, while an acceptance should make you feel proud, deserving, and successful, a rejection should never be taken personally.

In sum, applying to college is like going on a first date. You want to be honest about who you are. At the same time, you don't want to reveal anything less than positive about yourself. Wait until the relationship has reached a point where your flaws will be seen in the light of your many fine qualities. In other words, wait until you've been accepted and are living in your dorm.

Graduation

Twelve long years of school—worrying, struggling, hassling, dreading, hating, hoping, helping, longing, pleading, praying—and that's just what your parents have been through! No wonder they're so excited about their, er, your high school graduation.

This is the moment they've been waiting for. Free at last! No more tests. No more homework. No more meetings with the vice principal. Now they can sit back, relax, and look forward to...four more years?!!!

Graduation may be your triumph, but it's payback time for your parents. They'll be so giddy with pride and joy that they'll forget about the backpacks left on buses, the lost gym shorts, and the stolen sneakers. They won't remember the broken eyeglasses, the misplaced notebooks, and the report cards that never made it home.

In this delirious, all-is-forgiven state, they may do silly things. Like ask to be introduced to your friends. Or want to see your locker. Or insist that you stand on the school steps while they aim the camera, forget to remove the lens cap, re-aim the camera, focus, brush a fly from their forehead, re-aim the camera, tell everyone to smile, wait for your little brother to look, and then, with all 380 of your classmates watching, take a picture.

Yes, graduation is a day you'll always remember. To be sure it's a day you'll *want* to remember, here are some pointers for proper commencement behavior.

The Basics

SEND OUT INVITATIONS. Typically, these are provided by the school. They look something like this:

We, the Graduating Class
of Bedlam High School,
would be honored
to have you share our accomplishments
at Graduation
on Saturday, the 20th of May,
at one o'clock
in the High School Auditorium

If you just stick this in an envelope, the recipient will have no idea who the lucky graduate is. Therefore, include your card along with the invitation.

Mr. Chauncey Blunderbuster

What? No card? Then buy some blank ones. In your best scrawl, write your name by hand.

If you and several friends all want to invite the same person (for example, your soccer league coach), you may send one invitation. Just enclose all of your cards.

Because seating is usually limited at commencement exercises, you may not be able to invite as many people as you wish. In this case, you'll have to prioritize. Start with anyone likely to give you a car. Then invite your immediate family and closest relatives. If you still have some seats left, you can include mentors, friends, and distant relatives.

SEND OUT ANNOUNCEMENTS. These you send to friends and relatives who would be thrilled to hear of your accomplishments. This list might include tutors, coaches, piano teachers, scout leaders, and treasured baby-sitters from your childhood. If you had hoped to invite them to the graduation but were unable to do so because of limited seating, include a note to that effect. Let them know how much their support and/or friendship have meant to you over the years.

DON'T FISH FOR PRESENTS. It's tacky to stand on a street corner and hand out flyers about your graduation. Don't send invitations or announcements to the diaper service driver or the doctor who removed your tonsils—unless they went on to become your close friends.

BE TOLERANT OF PARENTS AND RELATIVES. Your folks will be bursting with pride. This means that they'll stalk you with a camcorder and reveal your family nickname ("Oh, Pooh-bear, we're so proud!"). They'll leave lipstick on your cheek and talk about you to anyone who will listen. Don't be embarrassed by your parents' behavior. Your friends have parents, too.

SHAKE, DON'T STIR. When you go up to receive your diploma, simply shake the principal's hand. No hugs, playful slugs on the shoulder, or European air kisses allowed.

THANK YOUR PARENTS. After all, you wouldn't be there if it weren't for them. In more ways than one.

The Finer Points

FOLLOW YOUR SCHOOL'S DRESS CODE WHEN DECIDING WHAT TO WEAR UNDER YOUR GOWN. You don't want to get sent home from your own graduation because of flip-flops or a belly-button ring. On the other hand, people at a graduation should pay attention to the speeches, not wonder what their classmates have on under their robes. So in theory, at least, it doesn't matter what you wear (or don't wear), as long as it doesn't set you apart from classmates who are properly attired. But I'd still recommend that dress-code thing.

UNDERSTAND THAT A GRADUATION IS NOT A PLACE TO PROTEST. Some adults get teary-eyed at the sight of a class of graduating seniors turning their backs on a distinguished speaker. For them, it evokes that Golden Age known as "The Sixties."

In fact, such behavior is *very* rude. Commencement exercises are group celebrations. They are not opportunities for individual expression. So it's no to the buttons, stickers, posters, placards, and pins.

Are there any exceptions to this rule? Rarely. Small ribbons, worn by group consent in loving memory of the 12 graduating seniors who were eaten by alligators on a field trip, would be one.

NEVER WALK OUT ON A SPEAKER. Some schools, to generate publicity or keep audiences awake, invite controversial people to speak at graduation. This might be someone who's been in the news, written a book, or just gotten out of jail. It might be someone you strongly disagree with or find personally offensive.

Too bad. Stay seated, keep quiet, and act like you're listening.

Remember that graduations are *group* exercises. Statements of personal belief—moral, political, or religious—by anyone other than the speaker are not appropriate. Booing, hissing, walking out, or wearing rabble-rousing slogans on your cap would all be breaches of etiquette. So would heckling, chanting, or talking during the speech.

Almost any speaker is sure to say *something* that *someone* disagrees with. Imagine the chaos if students shouted, stomped, strolled in and out, or bobbed up and down every time that happened.

To be brutally frank, the individual student and what he or she thinks don't count for beans at a graduation. This is a ceremony of, by, and for the community. It's for the families and the faculty; for tradition and knowledge; for the graduating class as a whole. You have a lifetime in which to express your opinions and fight for the causes of your choice. But until the ceremonies are over, keep a lid on—even if the speaker expresses beliefs that clash with your own.

There's one exception to this rule: hate speech. The more dignified your response is, the more power it will have. A quiet turning of backs or a solemn procession out of the auditorium would be a proper and restrained reaction. A student who stood up and said, "Sir (or Madam), these attacks are hateful, and they dishonor this institution and occasion. I must ask you to stop them," would forever be a hero in my book.

 **Do you have any tips for giving a valedictory address without offending anyone?**

Keep it short. Don't swear. Hurt no one. Tell a few inside jokes. Radiate idealism. Thank all parents and teachers. Don't trip when you leave the stage. ◆

A Brief History of Manners

Believe it or not, manners go back thousands of years. For a long time, humans were hunter-gatherers. They had to forage for food to keep from starving. This took a lot of energy and kept them on the road quite a bit, so they'd just grab a quick bite whenever they could.

Around 9000 B.C., people in the Near East figured out how to plant crops and farm. Now food could be grown, harvested, and stored. This led to a more stable existence and a lot less running around. As people began to eat together in families and groups, rituals evolved for preparing and sharing meals. These were then passed from one generation to the next.

The first known etiquette book—actually an "etiquette scroll"—was written around 2500 B.C. It was called *The Instructions of Ptahhotep* (after its Egyptian author), and it contained all sorts of advice for getting along with others and moving up in the world. This scroll was so widely read that many religious scholars believe its influence can be found in the Bible.

Before the 11th century, people in Europe ate with their fingers. A well-bred person used only three fingers—the thumb, the index finger, and the middle finger. You can imagine parents of that era saying, "Ethelred, how many times do I have to tell you? Don't stick your whole hand into your food!"

When forks were first used for eating in Tuscany (now part of Italy) in the 11th century, priests tried to make people stop using them. This was because food was seen as a gift from God. Only the human hand, another of God's creations, was fit to touch it. ("Ethelred, use your fingers, not your fork!")

The first stone knives were made some 1,500,000 years ago for slaughtering animals. By the Middle Ages, most men never left home without their knives. (Think of them as early cell phones, but sharper.) Knives were worn hung at the waist so they could be quickly drawn to kill an enemy or slice a steak.

This led to one of the biggest etiquette problems of the 17th century. Men would use the pointed ends of their knives to pick their teeth at the table. According to legend, this made the Duc de Richelieu go "Eewwwwwww!" He had all the points filed off the table knives in his chateau, and that's why the table knives we use today have blunt tips.

Etiquette books became popular in 13th-century Europe. They were written to instruct the upper classes on how to behave when invited to the royal court. These books contained gems like these:

When you blow your nose or cough, turn round so that nothing falls on the table.

Refrain from falling upon the dish like a swine while eating, snorting disgustingly, and smacking the lips.

Possibly the most influential etiquette book of all time was written in A.D. 1530 by Erasmus, a classical scholar who lived in Rotterdam. He believed that it was easiest to learn good manners in childhood. His book, *On Civility in Children,* became a huge bestseller and was required reading for kids throughout Europe for over two centuries. Here's some of his advice:

Turn away when spitting lest your saliva fall on someone.

Do not move back and forth in your chair. Whoever does that gives the impression of constantly breaking or trying to break wind.

You should not offer your handkerchief to anyone unless it has been freshly washed. Nor is it seemly, after wiping your nose, to spread out your handkerchief and peer into it as if pearls and rubies might have fallen out of your head.

If you look at old etiquette books, you can see that some manners have stayed the same over the centuries ("Don't spit on anyone"). Others have changed as the world has changed. For example, no one needed to know ten centuries ago that it's rude to talk on a cell phone during a movie. Fifty years from now, it may be rude to give your clone a noogie. Who knows?

Aren't manners just for snobs and rich people?

Not at all. Snobs have *bad* manners. By their attitude and behavior, they try to make others feel stupid and inferior. This is the height of rudeness. If people put you down for using the wrong fork, *they're* the ones with terrible manners, not you.

As far as rich people go, good manners are the one thing money can't buy. All you have to do is look around to realize that rudeness is an equal opportunity annoyer. That makes manners great equalizers. Anyone can learn them; anyone can use them. A poor person can be just as polite as a rich person—even more polite.

It's true that some rules of etiquette are more likely to be practiced by wealthier people—like tipping the wine steward, or setting a formal dinner table. And it seems that just because they have money, they can get away with bad manners in ways that others can't. But a nose being picked at the dinner table is disgusting, whether its owner is rich or poor. ◆

INDEX

ABOUT THE AUTHOR

Alex J. Packer (but you may call him "Alex") is a very polite educator and psychologist who only drinks from the carton if nobody's watching. He is the author of the award-winning *How Rude!*™ *The Teenagers' Guide to Good Manners, Proper Behavior, and Not Grossing People Out; HIGHS! Over 150 Ways to Feel Really, REALLY Good... Without Alcohol or Other Drugs; Bringing Up Parents: The Teenager's Handbook; Parenting One Day at a Time;* and other titles. His books have been translated into Spanish, German, and Chinese, although Alex says he can't tell if the Chinese version is really his book or a guide to lawnmower repair. His articles have appeared in *McCall's, Child, U.S. News and World Report,* and the *Harvard Graduate School of Education Bulletin.*

Alex prepped at Phillips Exeter Academy, where he never once referred to kitchen personnel as "wombats" (although he *was* told to get a haircut by his dorm master). He then went to Harvard, where he pursued a joint major in Social Relations and Finger Bowls, always striving to avoid classes on Mondays or Fridays. A specialist in adolescence, parent education, and substance abuse, Alex received a Master's Degree in Education from the Harvard Graduate School of (duh) Education, and a Ph.D. in Educational and Developmental Psychology from Boston College, where he held doors for his professors.

For eight years, Alex was headmaster of an alternative school for children ages 11–15 in Washington, D.C. He has since served as Director of Education for the Capital Children's Museum. He is currently President of FCD Educational Services, a leading Boston-based provider of drug education and prevention services for schools worldwide. When asking kids to not use drugs, Alex always says "please."

Although it's rude to talk behind someone's back, reliable sources report that Alex writes screenplays, spends several months a year in France, lives in a loft that used to be a pillow factory, and chews with his mouth closed.

Other Great Books from Free Spirit

How Rude!™

The Teenagers' Guide to Good Manners, Proper Behavior, and Not Grossing People Out
by Alex J. Packer, Ph.D.
Fourteen chapters describe the basics of polite behavior at home, in school, and in the world. Teens learn how to be a host with the most (and a guest with the best), what to do (and not to do) when going online or waiting in line, how to act at the mall and a concert hall, and much more. For ages 13 & up.
$19.95; 480 pp.; softcover; illus.; 7¼" x 9"

The How Rude!™ Handbook of Family Manners for Teens

by Alex J. Packer, Ph.D.
When family life is full of strife, what can a teen do? This book covers the basics of creating the civilized home—a place where people talk instead of yell, respect each other, fight fair, and don't hog the bathroom. Tips also cover the blended, shaken, stirred, and extended family, with special advice for teens whose parents are divorced. For ages 13 & up.
$9.95; 128 pp.; softcover; illus.; 5⅛" x 7"

The How Rude!™ Handbook of Friendship & Dating Manners for Teens

by Alex J. Packer, Ph.D.
Is there a proper way to make new friends? Is teasing always rude? How can you show a girl (or guy) that you like her (or him)? What's the best way to ask someone out...and who pays for the date? Teens learn the basics of polite behavior with friends and more-than-friends—and laugh out loud while learning. For ages 13 & up.
$9.95; 128 pp.; softcover; illus.; 5⅛" x 7"

School Power

Study Skill Strategies for Succeeding in School
Revised and Updated Edition
by Jeanne Shay Schumm, Ph.D.
This popular study-skills handbook, newly revised and updated, covers everything students need to know, including how to get organized, take notes, do Internet research, write better, read faster, study smarter, follow directions, handle long-term assignments, and more. For ages 11 & up.
$16.95; 144 pp.; softcover; illus.; 8½" x 11"

Too Stressed to Think?

A Teen Guide to Staying Sane When Life Makes You Crazy
by Annie Fox, M.Ed., and Ruth Kirschner
Most teens today are stressed out—family conflicts, school, friendship and dating issues, peer pressure, harassment, bullying, identity issues, anxiety, depression, alcohol, drugs, sex, and on and on. Questionnaires, exercises, role plays, and more help teens learn specific ways to relieve the stress in their lives. For ages 13 & up.
$14.95; 208 pp.; softcover; illus.; 6" x 9"

To place an order or to request a free catalog of
SELF-HELP FOR KIDS® and SELF-HELP FOR TEENS® materials,
please write, call, email, or visit our Web site:

Free Spirit Publishing Inc.
217 Fifth Avenue North • Suite 200 • Minneapolis, MN 55401-1299
toll-free 800.735.7323 • local 612.338.2068 • fax 612.337.5050
help4kids@freespirit.com • www.freespirit.com

What's faster, friendlier, and easier to use?

www.freespirit.com

New look · **New features** · **New sections** · **More ways to search** · **Quicker check-out** · **Stop in and see!**

Our fresh new Web site makes it easier than ever to find the positive, reliable resources you need to empower teens and kids of all ages.

The Catalog.
Start browsing with just one click.

Beyond the Home Page.
Information and extras such as links and downloads.

The Search Box.
Find anything superfast.

Your Voice.
See testimonials from customers like you.

Request the Catalog.
Browse our catalog on paper, too!

The Nitty-Gritty.
Toll-free numbers, online ordering information, and more.

The 411.
News, reviews, awards, and special events.

Our Web site is a secure commerce site. All of the personal information you enter at our site—including your name, address, and credit card number—is secure. So you can order with confidence when you order online from Free Spirit!

1.800.735.7323 • fax 612.337.5050 • help4kids@freespirit.com